AUSTRALIAN BIRDS

FOR BLUE – M. C.

AUSTRALIAN BIRDS

Artwork by
MATT CHUN

MAGPIE

Adult magpies have smooth black-and-white feathers but the chicks are fluffy and grey.

Although they can fly, they spend a lot of time on the ground looking for food. Many birds hop when they're not flying, but magpies walk along the ground with one foot in front of the other.

When they get hungry, they listen for insects moving in the soil and dig them up using their sharp beaks. They also eat plants and small animals.

Magpies often live together in big groups. They like to stay living in one place for their whole lives.

Magpies will sometimes swoop at people or animals that come too close to their nests, but only when the nests have chicks in them. They are usually quite tame and friendly.

Magpies can imitate other animals and even humans, but they are best known for their distinctive warbling song.

EASTERN YELLOW ROBIN

Eastern yellow robins are noisiest in the very early morning, making a bell-like piping call before the sun has risen. They live in a range of habitats, from parks and gardens to rainforests and dry woodland, and their bright flash of yellow feathers can often be seen when the birds perch sideways on tree trunks.

Eastern yellow robins don't eat plants, preferring to eat creatures such as spiders, ants, moths, flies and grasshoppers. When they are hunting, they usually perch on a low branch and swoop down onto their prey. They are very busy seeking out food from early in the morning until darkness falls. They mostly eat alone, but eastern yellow robins sometimes live and hunt in groups too. In winter, they will even forage with other types of insect-eating birds from time to time.

When they are ready to lay eggs, female birds build nests by weaving together different types of grasses and bark into a small cup-shape, and then they use spider webs to bind it together. Female birds keep the eggs warm, and their mates bring food to them as they sit on the nest. Both parents take care of the chicks once they hatch, sometimes with help from other birds in their group.

SUPERB FAIRY-WREN

Superb fairy-wrens live in flocks with one dominant male, a few younger males and a number of females. Female birds have brown feathers, as do young males. As they grow, male birds swap their dull brown feathers for iridescent blue plumage with patches of black and white. When this happens, male birds will sometimes pluck flower petals and show them to females to impress them. This bright new coat is not permanent, though – it only appears during breeding season, and changes back to brown for the rest of the year.

Superb fairy-wrens are not particularly shy, but they do like to live near plenty of dense, low cover that they can hide in if threatened. Female birds build their delicate, dome-shaped nests tucked away in low bushes. The female bird keeps the eggs warm, but both the male and female will take care of the chicks once they hatch, sometimes with help from other birds in the flock.

Although they can fly, superb fairy-wrens mostly hop along the ground on their spindly legs, generally only flying in short bursts.

They forage for food in groups, with some birds keeping a lookout as others hop jauntily along in search of food. Superb fairy-wrens eat a range of insects, including grasshoppers, ants, flies and beetles. They will also occasionally eat seeds, fruit and even flowers.

WEDGE-TAILED EAGLE

The wedge-tailed eagle is the largest bird of prey in Australia, with an enormous wingspan, powerful hooked bill and legs that are surprisingly long and feathery.

They live in open country and forested areas, maintaining the same territory over their lifetime. They generally build their nests in very tall trees. Their gigantic nests are built using dead sticks and can weigh up to 300kg! Although nest shapes can vary, they all have a hollow cup-shape at the top where the eggs are laid. Both parents share nest-building duties and they also both keep the eggs warm and feed the chicks once they hatch. Interestingly, the eggs are not all laid at once. Each individual egg is laid with a gap of a few days in between, which means the chicks hatch a few days apart.

Chicks are covered with white downy feathers when they hatch, and their first feathers are a reddish brown. Plumage becomes darker with age, with adult birds having dark brown to black feathers. Female birds are generally larger than males, and slightly paler too.

Wedge-tailed eagles eat both live prey and dead animals. They mostly eat rabbits, but also hunt animals such as hares, wallabies, lizards and birds. They can hunt alone, but also in pairs or larger groups. When working together, groups of wedge-tailed eagles can catch larger prey such as kangaroos. Wedge-tailed eagles use warm currents of air to reach extraordinary heights, where they will circle and glide as they look for prey.

RAINBOW LORIKEET

Rainbow lorikeets live in areas with plenty of trees, including woodlands, rainforests and urban areas. They generally keep to one place, but will travel to find food.

Rainbow lorikeets feed mostly on pollen and nectar, but also eat seeds, fruit and insects. Their tongues are long and agile with a brush-shape on the end, which allows them to reach inside blossoms and pick up pollen and nectar with ease. They usually forage in small groups, but can also gather in much larger flocks when there is an abundance of food. They forage throughout the day, and then roost in trees overnight. They can be quite noisy birds, making regular screeching and chattering calls.

As you can guess by the name, rainbow lorikeets have remarkably bright plumage. Although there is some variation between birds, each one usually has a vivid blue head and underbelly, with green feathers along their wings, tail and back, and a splash of orange and yellow on their chest. Young birds have black beaks, which become orange as they get older.

Rainbow lorikeets build their nests in tree hollows, lining them with wood shavings. Both parents build the nest and feed the chicks once they hatch, but only the mother keeps the eggs warm.

AUSTRALIAN PELICAN

Pelicans will live just about anywhere with open water and plenty of food, from urban parks to coastal lagoons. They are the heaviest flying bird in Australia. Instead of using up energy by flapping their broad wings, they use warm air currents to glide to incredible heights in the sky.

Pelicans mostly eat fish, using their sensitive bills to find them underwater and scoop them up. Their bills have a slightly hooked end, which helps them hold onto slippery prey. They also eat many other animals that live near water, including waterbirds and their eggs, yabbies and even turtles.

Even though the pouch under a pelican's bill is very roomy, they don't store food in it – they prefer to swallow things whole as they catch them. Sometimes groups of pelicans will work together, herding groups of fish into shallow water where they are easier to catch.

Their long bills are usually pale pink and yellow, but turn bright pink, blue and yellow for a short time just before their eggs are laid. Once the eggs are in the nest, both parents use their big feet to keep them warm until they hatch. Large groups of pelicans will often nest together in one place. Pelican chicks are very odd-looking birds, with bumpy, mottled skin, bulging eyes and oversized bills.

POWERFUL OWL

Powerful owls hunt at night, sometimes in pairs or family groups. During the day they sleep in trees. Powerful owls usually live in forest and woodland areas, and they like to stay living in one place.

They are the largest owls in Australia, and they have enormous feet with powerful talons. When they hunt, they use these talons to catch their prey as they swoop down from the treetops with incredible speed.

They eat a wide range of animals, including possums and gliders, as well as birds, rabbits, bats, insects and even koalas. Sometimes after hunting, a powerful owl will wait to eat the food that it has caught until the next night. It will perch on a tree branch and sleep through the day, holding its catch between the branch and its claw.

Male birds build nests inside the hollows of old trees. They bring food to their mate as she keeps the eggs warm, and they also deliver food for the chicks once they hatch. A pair of powerful owls will mate for life.

Unlike many other types of owl, male powerful owls are bigger than females, although both have similar feather patterns and large piercing eyes.

LAUGHING KOOKABURRA

Laughing kookaburras are territorial birds that live in the same place for their entire lives. They like to live in woodland areas with plenty of large trees for nesting and open areas where they can hunt for food.

Laughing kookaburras are a particularly large type of kingfisher. They get their name from their distinctive call, which sounds like raucous laughter. They use this song to mark their territory, and groups of kookaburras will often sing at once in chorus. Laughing kookaburras are most often heard in the morning and evening, but they sing at all times of the day.

Laughing kookaburras stay with the same mate once they have found each other, and they also live in family groups. Even after they have grown up, chicks stay with their families. They build their nests in tree hollows, sometimes using the hollows created by termites. Males and females keep the eggs warm in the nest, and they both take care of the chicks too, sometimes with help from other birds in their group.

Laughing kookaburras eat many kinds of insects, as well as frogs, birds and even small snakes or mammals. They often sit on a branch to look out for prey, and once they spot something suitable they will pounce down and snatch it up in their large beaks.

AUSTRALIAN BRUSH TURKEY

Brush turkeys are clumsy flyers and spend most of their time on the ground, only flying to escape predators or roost in trees. They mostly eat fruit that has fallen to the ground, as well as seeds and insects.

Brush turkeys lay their eggs in a very strange way. The male builds a large mound out of leaves and twigs. Sometimes these mounds are as big as a car! Many different female birds will lay eggs inside each mound, which means the mounds can have as many as 50 eggs inside. Female birds leave after laying their eggs, and the male looks after them. He sticks his beak into the mound to check the temperature regularly. The mound needs to be warm enough to hatch the eggs, but not hot enough to cook them. He takes off leaves to cool down the eggs, or adds more if the mound isn't warm enough inside.

When the eggs hatch, the chicks have to dig their way out of the mound. They have feathers as soon as they hatch, and can fly as soon as they dry off.

Brush turkeys have a fleshy bunch of skin under their throats called a 'wattle', which can be blue or yellow.

EASTERN ROSELLA

Eastern rosellas are very colourful birds, with vivid red feathers on their heads, white spots on their cheeks and a mix of blue, green, yellow and black plumage on the rest of their bodies.

Young eastern rosellas have dull feathers that brighten as they age. Their beaks also change colour as they get older, turning from yellow and orange to white.

Eastern rosellas often live together in small groups, and when they find a mate they stay with them for life. They make different calls when they are flying or perched in trees and can be quite vocal.

Eastern rosellas usually prefer to live in areas with lots of tall eucalypt trees. This can include more remote, forested areas as well as urban parks and gardens. They are native to the south-east of Australia.

They generally nest in the hollows of tall trees and often return to the same nest year after year. Female birds keep the eggs warm, and male birds bring food to their mates as they sit on the nest.

Eastern rosellas eat many different seeds, fruits, berries and buds, as well as nectar and blossoms. They also eat insects and their larvae.

GALAH

Pink-and-grey galahs are a type of cockatoo. They are social, playful birds that live in large flocks. They nest in tree hollows lined with leaves, so they like to live in places with plenty of big trees.

Galahs eat many different kinds of seeds, which they usually forage for on the ground. They often travel long distances in search of food and they can fly as fast as a car.

Pink-and-grey galahs roost high in the treetops when they sleep, and return to the same spot to sleep night after night. During the heat of the day, large, noisy groups will also take a break from looking for food to rest in treetops.

Galahs mate for life and form very strong bonds with each other. Male and female birds both keep the eggs warm in the nest. Pink-and-grey galahs will occasionally breed with other types of cockatoo, including the sulphur-crested cockatoo.

Male and females look the same, with their eye colour one of the only ways to tell them apart. Males have dark brown or black eyes and females have red eyes, but it can be hard to tell the difference unless you are very close.

TAWNY FROGMOUTH

Tawny frogmouths can live happily in many different habitats, from woodlands to urban areas. They hunt at night and sleep perched on branches during the day, choosing trees that match their feather patterns so they can blend in and stay safe from predators. When they stay still and keep their striking yellow eyes closed, they look like part of a branch.

Tawny frogmouths are often mistaken for owls, but they are very different. They have extra-wide bills with hooked tips, and they don't have strong talons like many other birds of prey. This means that instead of using their feet when they hunt, tawny frogmouths catch most of their prey using their large beaks.

Tawny frogmouths like to eat insects, as well as spiders, frogs, reptiles and small birds or mammals. They pounce down from perches in trees to catch their prey. They also keep their mouths open when they sleep so that they can catch any unsuspecting insects that might wander inside. In the cold winter months, tawny frogmouths can make their heartbeats and metabolisms slow down to save energy.

Tawny frogmouths build twiggy, platform-like nests high in trees, and both parents keep the eggs warm and feed the chicks once they hatch. They usually lay eggs at the same time each year, but sometimes they will also lay eggs as a response to heavy rains.

SOUTHERN CASSOWARY

Southern cassowaries live in dense rainforest. Each bird lives alone and keeps to the same territory for their whole lives. They can't fly, but they can run extraordinarily fast, jump high in the air and even swim. The vivid blue skin on their head and neck is brighter on female birds and changes colour with their mood. The tough, helmet-like bump, called a 'casque', on the top of their head keeps growing over time.

They are shy birds, but can become aggressive when under threat – hissing and kicking out with the long, dagger-like claws on their powerful feet. They also make deep rumbling and booming sounds when protecting their territory.

Male birds build the nests, and after laying large, green eggs the female will leave the father to keep them warm. It takes around 50 days for the eggs to hatch, and during this time the father will stay on the nest, rarely eating or drinking.

Southern cassowaries mostly eat fruit off the forest floor, but also eat fungi, snails and even small dead animals. They can eat fruit whole, even if it is very large, which means that entire fruit seeds are left in their droppings. This helps distribute the seeds over large areas, enabling the rainforest to grow and regenerate.

The southern cassowary is endangered, mostly due to habitat loss, and only lives in a handful of areas in Northern Queensland.

SUPERB LYREBIRD

Superb lyrebirds live in forested areas. They can fly, but their wings are quite small and weak so they spend most of their time on the ground. They perch in trees to sleep so that they will be safe from predators.

Superb lyrebirds find food by scratching through leaf litter with their strong feet. They eat spiders, worms, snails, frogs and seeds.

Both male and female lyrebirds have a long tail, but the male's is much more ornate, with curved feathers that can be fanned out in a stunning display. During mating season, males build mounds within their territory and then prance and strut on top of them, extending their tail feathers and making a complex singing call. The superb lyrebird is known for its incredibly diverse song, which includes imitations of other birds and sounds created by humans, such as musical instruments and phone ringtones. This song can be heard at any time of year, but is much more common when male birds are trying to attract a mate. Superb lyrebirds learn most of their songs from older males rather than picking them up directly from their surroundings.

When it is time to lay eggs, female lyrebirds build a dome-shaped nest and line it with soft materials, including feathers, moss and ferns. They generally only lay one egg, and the mother takes care of the chick alone.

SULPHUR-CRESTED COCKATOO

When sulphur-crested cockatoos gather in large flocks, their raucous screeching can be overwhelming. They generally live in large groups, and regularly preen each other's feathers. The bold yellow crest of feathers on their heads can sit folded back in a plume or extended out like a mohawk.

Many birds produce an oil to keep their feathers dry, but sulphur-crested cockatoos produce a fine, white powder from their feathers for waterproofing. As they preen their feathers, their black beaks become coated with powder and often look grey as a result. Their incredibly sharp beaks are also used to crack open seed shells so that they can use their long, agile tongues to scoop out the seed kernels inside. Sulphur-crested cockatoos also eat nuts, roots, berries and insects and their larvae. Flocks of birds fly back to the same food source each day until it has been cleared out. When they are feeding, some birds keep a lookout and warn the others if any threats are approaching.

When they are not eating, sulphur-crested cockatoos will often roost together in trees, nipping and peeling at the bark and branches to keep their beaks sharp.

They build their nests in tree hollows, and both parents keep the eggs warm and feed the chicks. Even after they have grown, sulphur-crested cockatoo chicks keep on living with their parents.

EMU

Emus generally prefer to live in open areas of grassland. They don't usually stay in one place for long, as they travel long distances each day seeking out food. Emus mostly eat plants, but will also eat insects and small animals. They like to eat the most nutritious parts of plants such as the fruit, shoots and young leaves, and avoid parts that are old or dried out. They swallow stones to help grind up food during digestion.

Emus are one of the tallest birds in the world, and they're very heavy too. They have tiny wings and cannot fly, but they can run as fast as a car on their long, powerful legs and are surprisingly strong swimmers. They have a second set of eyelids that are clear and move from side to side, which helps to keep out dust.

Emus, particularly females, mark their territory with a booming call. They also make a deep drumming sound during mating season.

Emu eggs are bright green when they are first laid, but soon become much darker. Female emus leave after laying eggs and the male bird keeps them warm alone. It takes about 50 days for emu eggs to hatch, and the male bird will stay sitting on the nest for this entire time. They can't eat or drink on the nest, so they can become very weak and thin during this time. When the chicks hatch, they are small enough to fit in a human hand, and have downy feathers with brown-and-cream stripes.

Little Hare Books
an imprint of
Hardie Grant Children's Publishing
Wurundjeri Country
Level 11, 36 Wellington Street
Collingwood Victoria 3066
Melbourne | Sydney | San Francisco
hardiegrant.com/childrens

First published 2018

A catalogue record for this book is available from the National Library of Australia

Hardie Grant acknowledges the Traditional Owners of the country on which we work, the Wurundjeri people of the Kulin nation and the Gadigal people of the Eora nation, and recognises their continuing connection to the land, waters and culture. We pay our respects to their Elders past and present.

978 1 760502 00 3 (hbk.)

Designed by Pooja Desai
Text by Ella Meave
Produced by Pica Digital, Singapore
Printed in China by Leo Paper Group

10 9 8 7 6 5